# Walking Upon High Places

## Yolanda C Holmes

© 2018 Yolanda Holmes

All Scriptures, quotations are taken from the KING JAMES VERSION (KJV): KING JAMES VERSION, public domain.

Published by:
Yolanda Holmes
P.O. Box 131
Wichita Falls, TX 76307

All rights reserved. No part of this publication may be reproduced stored in a retrieval system, or transmitted in any form or by any means-electronic, mechanical, photocopy, recording, or any other-without the prior written permission of the publisher. For permission contact:

holmescyolanda@gmail.com

Edited by Ruth

Pictures Provided by:
Michelle Ferguson and Isis Holmes

Printed in the United States of America

Table of Contents

| | |
|---|---|
| Foreward | 6 |
| Making the decision | 9 |
| Preparing for the journey | 19 |
| Knowing your obstacles | 27 |
| Strength in Numbers | 41 |
| Mental Strength | 49 |
| Balance | 61 |
| Your Responsibility | 69 |
| What if...? | 72 |
| The View | 80 |

To my wonderful husband, Wesley
Who has supported me from day one, and has been my silent pillar.
To my beautiful children Whitney, Big Whit, Isis, Heavenah, Wesley III, Malachi Anaiah and Zoe. You all are such a blessing!
Thank You for your support and patience.
I Love You

# Chapter 2
# Foreword

A while back I remember being handed a little sheet of paper that asked me questions, it caused me to dig deep within myself. The questions were there to help me find out what gifts, talents, and areas of my life that could be useful in the ministry.

Since then I've realized that the Lord has called me to a mighty work, and out of all the things that I have been through in my life I now know He's been preparing me my whole life.

This book has been written to use as a tool that will help you to walk the path that was predestinated for you. You will gain more insight of your adversary and his tricks, and by the end of the book, you should notice your growth.

*And we know that all things
work together for good
to them that love God, to them
who are the called according to his
purpose. For whom he did foreknow,
he also did predestinate to be
conformed to the image of his Son,
that he might be the firstborn among
many brethren. Moreover whom he
did predestinate, them he also
called:
and whom he called,
them he also justified: and
whom he justified,
them he also glorified.
Romans 8:28-30*

## Chapter 3

## Making the decision to walk on high places

### 3 Steps to begin your Journey

1. You have the feeling that there is something more to life
2. Acknowledge
3. Obedience

### The Itch

Have you ever felt that there is something more to your life, but you've found yourself hesitating to move forward? I call this an itch! This itch is what you find yourself daydreaming about at random times. Even if you're prospering in your current position, there always seems to be this little something that keeps nudging you. People that are close to you know about your dream (the itch), because you've shared it with them. Sometimes you've even given up talking about it because it doesn't seem to be happening. You've lost hope, and you feel miserable because you've buried it in the back of your mind, so you don't have to deal with it. To no surprise, it always shows back up. Maybe this itch is singing, teaching, mentoring, mission work, evangelizing, or preaching. Whatever the itch is it's time to do something about it!

    Acknowledging the itch means that you're bringing it to the surface, so it's no longer in hiding. It will no longer have this silent stronghold over you.

You have a calling my friend, and it's not going to go away. The reason it doesn't go away is because someone needs what you have! You've been handpicked and equipped for your calling. Your calling is something that the Lord has blessed you with to help fulfill His overall purpose of serving others.

## Obedience

*[handwritten: Singing/music]*

Now that you have acknowledged you have a calling being obedient is the next step. Obedience is demonstrating the willing attitude to comply with what's expected.

Getting to the point of obedience at first can be a bit fearful, but keep in mind that obedience is better than sacrifice (1 Samuel 15:22). I remember having a conversation with a friend, and she was telling me how she needed to fast, so she wanted to give this and that up to please God. My friend is a person I know that has a gift to fulfill a purpose to serve. However, she keeps running from it. This conversation was becoming draining by the minute. I can only take so much before I speak up, so when my friend stopped talking, I was able to ask her a simple question. "<u>Have you done what you were supposed to?</u>" In so many words the answer was no, with excuse after excuse. Using the example of a child, I asked her; if a child is asked to do something by a parent, does the child neglect what the parent says and does the opposite? The parent may tell the child to eat their vegetables but rather than doing what's instructed they choose to eat candy, or not at all. What the child doesn't realize is that the parent sees the overall picture. To do the opposite than what you're instructed shows that we are leaning on our own understanding. With this type of thinking, we get nowhere. We can sacrifice all day long thinking we're getting closer to God, but because of disobedience, the sacrifice is no good. Many people start their calling then begin sliding and falling before they've even taken off, because of what they think they know. Understand that we serve a God of order. Jesus came that we may have life and there is freedom in Jesus, but when we do it out of order, we are wrong. Your sacrifice is not nearly what your obedience should be. Stop making excuses and do it! If God has placed something in your heart and it won't go away, there is a reason for that. Stop thinking whatever you're doing is replacing what you should be doing. Get your thoughts out of it and release it to your heavenly Father.

*I must work the works of him
that sent me, while it is day:
the night cometh, when no
man can work. John 9:4*

    Maybe you plan on being obedient, but you have concluded that you're waiting for the right time. I've given a name to this particular time in life. I call it lingering! You're not moving in the direction you're supposed to be going, but you have plans to. I know this so well because I've been a victim of it for many different reasons, so this is more common than you think. It has happened many times in the bible.

    Until you've realized that His plan for you is above anything you can imagine, you're only able to go so far. You must know that your thoughts for yourself are small compared to His. It's time to give up the fight and surrender. You never really know as much as you think. This way of thinking comes with being in the world. It's time to wake up! You are His vessel, so it's time to break the cycle of events in your life that keep hindering you! You must step out of what you know.

I'm reminded of a man who lingered a little bit too long, and when he finally did leave he wanted to go his own way because of what he thought. In Genesis 18 Abraham makes intercessor for Lot because Lot is living in a city that God is very unhappy with, so Abraham is having a conversation with God because God is getting ready to destroy Sodom and Gomorrah(Genesis 18:20). You find that Abraham is talking to the Lord and asking Him if there are 50 righteous, please do not destroy it, but Abraham doesn't stop at fifty he continues to bring this number down until it reaches ten. The Lord responds if there are ten he will not destroy it. Genesis 18:33. Well, this brings us up to Lot. Chapter 19 Lot and his wife and two daughters are living in the city, and the Lord sends two angels to Sodom and Gomorrah. They are sent there to tell Lot that they are there to destroy the place and he and his family will need to leave. After hearing this from the angels, Lot lingers around, rather than getting his wife and daughters and fleeing to the mountains.

Sometimes we want to remain in what we know for a lot of different reasons. Regardless of the reason, we've become too comfortable in our situation, and what you've been around for a long time. We don't even realize that we are dependent on our environment. Maybe you've been warned about moving, but have continued to procrastinate. Think about where you could be right now, and what's passing you by the longer you're lingering in the present situation. Has God placed something on your heart, but you're staying too long? Don't let something happen to have to move you by force. <u>Submit and be willing to make the change.</u> If you read further down in the scripture, you'll learn the angels gave them instruction not to stay in the plains but run for the mountains. The warning came again, but they didn't listen, it took force. They eventually fled to the plains, but not where they were supposed to go (the mountains). I've asked myself why he couldn't just go the place he was supposed to. Well, I've been guilty also, and sometimes wanted to put my two cents in rather than do as instructed. I've concluded this happens because of what I'm around and how I've gotten so caught up in life that I forget that I'm not God. That's a big wakeup call! Well, Lot and his wife and daughters left but before they were entirely out of danger, his wife looked back and then she turned into a pillar of salt. Okay, don't look back too soon once you've made the decision, keep moving forward.

How can we get to the Mountain we're called to go to when we haven't let go of what we know and stop procrastinating? If you read the rest of the story, it will go on to say what happens to Lot and his daughters. Remember he now has no wife and the devastating choices his daughters will make all came from the environment he had his family in.

Your environment affects your decisions.

You must remember this is a faith walk you're on.

## Chapter 4
## Preparing for the journey

Now that you've done the three steps in the previous chapter, it's now time to make the preparations for where you're heading. I'm going to compare this journey to mountain climbing because there's a lot of similarity between the two. They both require extensive preparation for the mental, emotional, and physical strength. You don't attempt to climb a mountain without studying the best route. The same with your spiritual journey don't expect it to take off and make it to the top being unprepared. You will have to prepare. Let's not make the common mistake and start slipping because of lack of preparation. Get ready to start packing your bag for the journey, so that you will make for a good ending! You will start out with three of the most important lessons you can learn.

**Lesson One**

You're excited right now, and your mind is racing a hundred miles an hour and you want to share this with everyone you know. You feel like posting it for the whole world to know that the King has chosen you. Being a vessel of the Lord is truly exciting, but you can't tell everyone. Listen! You've made one of the most significant decisions of your life, and deciding to answer your call is a big deal! However, along with that excitement, there is also fear, and anxiety all bundled up. I understand how important this is to you, but regardless of your emotions right now you must be careful who you tell. Everyone is not for you! There are some out there who want to destroy you before you even begin. The negativity can become so great that if you're not careful, you will start to feel pressured to the point of becoming defeated before you start. I call this pressure overload. You must remember that there is an adversary out to get you, and his purpose is to kill, steal, and destroy you on this journey. Something as precious as you're calling should be handled delicately. The time will come soon enough where everyone will know it. Give yourself some time to build "you" up! Practice becoming wise with what you tell people. If you were to get a million dollars today would you want to tell everyone? Personally, I wouldn't because I know people would be coming to see what they could get from me. I would only share information with those I trust in my life. There should be people in your life that you know right now that you could trust with delicate information, like this. These people you know should love God, and for you and your journey.

Being wise is essential to this season in your life.

A scripture to meditate on was when Jesus was talking to His disciples he instructed them to be wise as a serpent and harmless as a dove (Matthew 10:16).

**Lesson Two**

Have you ever packed for a camping/hiking trip, or any trip that involves being outside? In preparing for this trip do you go without a tent? Probably not; when I think of camping, I think of being out in the woods. As I'm preparing my bags, I'm wondering about all the equipment that I will need to be safe outside and to make this trip possible. To be out in the middle of nowhere, you can't pack any bag; you'll need something to sleep on as well as something to heat up food. Now just as you would pack a bag in the natural with equipment for your journey, you will also have to pack your bag in the spiritual preparing for your spiritual journey. First and foremost you're going to have to spend time with the Lord. Quality time is not just on the go, but clearing a part of your day just for Him. Keeping in mind that this is something you will have to schedule in. It will seem that everything will pop up when you have made this decision, but remain steadfast. This time is so essential because if you don't have a relationship with the Lord, you have no way of knowing who He is. How will you receive your instruction if you don't know His voice? To be in the presence of the Lord is a feeling that you will long for after you've begun to do it. You will find that in His presence He'll visit you and order your steps. He is the master planner, so put Him first in everything, and He's going to guide and direct you in exactly what to do. Don't go by what you know (we tend to mess it all up), but remember this is a walk of faith. Trust Him for every direction and every detail of your journey. Knowing your course means you're going to have to learn to listen, and you're going to have to study. Putting time in with the Lord will make for confidence in your directions. Many have started, but few only remain, because of their lack of preparation. When stopping has become an option, then it's because of lack of development or doing what's needed. Being faithful will mean you're going to do this regardless of what comes up. You're determined and ready for your journey.

**Lesson Three**

Now that you're wise on what you share with others, and you're spending quality time with the Lord. Let's talk about studying.

*2 Timothy 2:15*
*Study to shew thyself approved unto God,*
*a workman that needeth not to be ashamed*
*rightly dividing the word of truth.*

It's necessary to attend biblical studies and also to study on your own looking for things to challenge your mind while diving into the word of God. You want to be found studying the word of God because the word of God is a map. It has the plans that you need to succeed. It's part of your armor that's essential to your faith. Learning the promises of God, so that you can share this with others because of no matter what field you're in or whatever you're calling this is necessary to know. The purpose you have to serve in the body of Christ is what you are preparing for; don't be caught without what you need. He loves you and sent his only begotten son to die on the cross for you so that you may have a chance to eternal life. Learn and stand on the gospel because at the end of the day you must stay focused on the basics of why the calling is there. Knowing that what you're doing is not about you, but all about His purpose. It's not about success or fame, but it's all about the people he has placed in your path to be a witness to. If you start off with your focus wrong, you won't get very far. We give room for the devil to begin early in the ministry. Get your view right! You're a vessel, and any other reason that you are doing this except for the kingdom is wrong.

Chapter 5
Knowing your obstacles

**Understanding what's involved**

Now that you're prepared for the journey you will be facing obstacles along the way. An obstacle is something that poses a barrier to hinder progress. Certain barriers that can stop you! These are the barriers that satan will use as trickery. However, God allows these things to be in the way for a reason;

they will make you stronger in the end.

> *But as for you, ye thought evil against me;*
> *but God meant it unto good,*
> *Genesis 50:20*

### Denial

Denial is refusing to admit the truth or the reality of something. We are reminded daily of people all around us who are walking in denial. When denial is present, there is a defense that's always up. There will be a verbal justification that will support their defense mode. Denial is a terrible place to be in because it puts people in a vulnerable state, and in this fragile state they've become blinded to the truth. They are in constant battle in their mind. Here are some examples to watch out for to see if denial has its claws in you.  There could be something or someone hurting you, or it could be a negative family member who is always barking at what you can't do. However, you keep accepting it because you love them. Maybe it's the friend you have continued to let lead you to things that you later regret, but instead of dismissing them you keep saying they're going to change. Perhaps it's the thoughts you are struggling with but don't want to tell anyone what's happened, so you keep it bottled up telling yourself you are strong. When in reality your up at night thinking, and struggling because of nightmares. It's the anger you don't want to face, but you keep flying off the handle. Not wanting to acknowledge that there is a root to your bitterness, anger, and rage.

      Denial needs to be laid down. It's time to stop making

excuses and surrender whatever is preventing you from producing the fruit the Lord has for you. Here is a scripture for prayer and meditation to use while asking the Lord to bring it to the surface if you're battling with denial. You will need to renounce this spirit that has taken control and ask the Lord to forgive you.

*Thus saith the Lord cursed be the man that trusteth in man, and maketh flesh his arm and whose heart departeth from the Lord. For he shall be like the heath in the desert, and shall not see when good cometh; but shall inhabit the parched places in the wilderness, in a salt land and not inhabited. Blessed is the man that trusteth in the Lord, and whose hope the Lord is. For he shall be as a tree planted by the waters, and that spreadeth out her roots by the river,*

*and shall not see when heat cometh but her leaf shall be green; and shall not be careful in the year of drought, neither shall cease from yielding fruit.*
*Jeremiah 17:5-8*

When you are living in denial and putting your trust and faith in man, it will show. It will show whom you've chosen to serve. You won't have to say much because when we're living for the Lord and have surrendered everything to Him, you will be as a tree planted by the river. You will bloom because you will have your supply. You won't be as the Heath lacking and not growing. It's time to make a choice either to be as a flourishing called child of God or to be as one who will remain a runt.

**Things we know**

Knowing too much is also a huge obstacle that gets in the way. In the Bible, you read about a man by the name of Nicodemus he was a ruler of the Jews. John 3:1-12 tells how this ruler goes to Jesus by night telling Jesus that he knows that He is a teacher sent by God, because of the things that he was doing is evidence that God is with Him. Jesus tells Nicodemus unless a man is born again he cannot see the kingdom of God. Nicodemus' thought process only takes him so far, and he is hindered by what he knows, not being able to grasp what Jesus is telling him. He begins to wonder how an old man can enter the womb again. This is an example of knowledge stopping you from being open to truth. This response shows the shallowness we have when we lean on what we know. There will be a lot of things that don't look like it makes sense, but if you're following the Lord's direction; know that it doesn't have to look normal to work out. We are peculiar people and have to get out of the worldly mindset.

Remember Lot; he figured he had a good enough excuse why he went to the plains rather than the mountains. The "all knowing" attitude will prevent progress. Stop thinking you've got it all figured out, it's time to trust Him! The next time you feel that you've got the answer pray about it first. Make it a practice to pray before you act. Consult your Saviour, because He's already worked it out.

**Busyness**

Don't think for one moment, now that you while you are on your journey you're not going to have a to-do list. Things you've been putting off for a while will start to show up, and things you've forgotten about will also come up. People will need you for everything and require your input on everything. You may get that demanding promotion you've desired for a long time. You need to be prepared if this happens. God is first, spouse, children, and then your job. Always be ready and know whatever decisions you make line it up with that order. If it takes away from God's order, it'll be a hindrance. You don't have to say "no" to everything, but you need to set boundaries to do God's work freely. Freely doing God's work isn't being consumed by a task that will lead you to be distracted from God's plans. The story in the bible that comes to mind is the one of Martha and Mary (Luke 10:38-42). Martha receives Jesus in her home. Martha has a sister by the name of Mary who chooses to sit at the feet of Jesus and to hear his words. Meanwhile, her sister Martha is busy trying to do everything she thought was required for serving, so she went to Jesus and asked Him to tell her sister to help her since she left her by herself doing everything. Jesus answered and told her about herself and that what her sister was doing was what was needed and he wasn't going to take that from her. Wow, wakeup call! When we think we have to do it all Jesus is there to remind us to do what's needed.

### Fear

Fear can be part of denial because fear keeps us from moving forward. It seems to creep up anytime something new is about to happen. Have you ever felt butterflies in your stomach on the first day of school as a kid? You don't want to go, but you know your parents aren't going to back down. If you could, you would've stayed at home where you feel safe. That's how we can get over the fear. Fear causes us to want to stay in what's comfortable rather than take a risk. There are times in life that you'll want to back out and not move forward. You are afraid because you don't know the outcome. You have all types of questions that if said to others it sounds a bit absurd. You must remember the Lord has it and that calling that you feel is because He has equipped you. He knows your heart and already has predestined your destiny. Let the fear go, and don't let it consume you. Joshua was called to lead the children of Israel into Jordan. God commands Joshua saying.

> *"Have not I commanded thee?*
> *Be strong and of good courage;*
> *be not afraid, neither be thou*
> *dismayed:*

*for the Lord thy God is with thee whithersoever thou goest*
*Joshua 1:9*

We must know that He is with us wherever He instructs us to go. To know His will should give you peace.

**Curveballs**

The next obstacle is curve balls; this is one of the most significant obstacles that if you are not alert and watchful, this will cause you to lose focus to the point of destruction. A Curveball is a ball that is thrown by the pitcher that curves and doesn't go straight to the batter. The curve will make it nearly impossible for the batter to hit the ball. It's unexpected, and usually, the batter is not ready. However, this one right here can knock you off your feet if you're not watchful.

I want to talk to you about King David, the man after Gods own heart. David was instructed to bring the arc back to Jerusalem, so he gathers a crew of chosen men of Israel, and they are to bring the arc back to Jerusalem (2 Samuel chapter 6). David has this group of man who builds a new cart to hold the arc. Everyone is excited especially about this move, so the arc is going back to where it belongs. David and all the house of Israel are playing instruments and praising the Lord. During this time one of the men (Uzzah) stretched forth his hand to touch the arc and immediately he falls dead. There were specific instructions on transporting this arc that was not followed through. Scripture says that David became displeased with the Lord, because of what the Lord had done. David was shaken to the core that he became afraid of the Lord that he left the arc alone. David stopped his journey for three months because this unexpected event (curveball) knocked him off his feet. I can only imagine the questions he had in his head. This story is an eye-opener: It shows that it doesn't matter about your title curve balls can happen to anyone.

You can be facing things in life that will shake you while you are heading to your destination. Even though David paused, he later finds out that just because he took a break doesn't mean God stops His blessings. The house the arc was left in began to reap the blessings of God. When David heard of this, it motivated him to get back on track. The Lord's work must get done regardless, so if it's not you, it will be somebody. Just because you've been thrown a curve ball doesn't mean you need to quit! Quitting is the easy way out. Whatever the curveball may be it will hurt, you may slow down to grasp the situation. Whatever you do remember not to stop doing what you're supposed to completely, the Lord has entrusted you to complete a job, and you must continue. Press forward; you're not the only one who has been hit. David shows us that it can happen to anyone.

Obstacles come in many different forms. There are some that aren't even listed. These are just a few that I know to be prevalent in people's lives today. Satan's job is to try to stop you, but you must remember that this journey is not easy. If that were the case, then everyone would be doing it. Ask the Lord to open your eyes, so you will be able to discern in your life. He's faithful to do it, and when you feel weary and beaten down take a moment to remember who God is. Sometimes you need a break to reflect on who God is to you.

Chapter 6
Strength in Numbers

**Support System**

In chapter two I informed you that it was okay to share your calling with people that support you by their prayers and encouraging words.

Having a support system is essential; The Lord will never send a soldier into battle alone. The Lord has some people just for you. In 1 Kings 19:4-14 Elijah is sitting under a Juniper tree asking the Lord to take his life because all of the prophets had been slain, and he was the only one left. Even though Elijah wanted to die, the Lord was not through with him yet. The Lord sent an angel to feed him and after which he traveled to Horeb the mountain of God. It was inside of a cave on this mountain; the Lord spoke to Elijah asking him. "What are you doing here?" It's clear that Elijah was not where he needed to be. From reading this text, you may want to ask yourself why God allowed him to run when he was supposed to be somewhere else. In life when we have headed in a direction that we were not supposed to when things started happening, so we got weary and a little bit afraid. We run or turnaround because we're facing the things that we don't understand. What's happening is its unfolding right up under our eyes. This is not the time to run this is the time to stand. Elijah responds by explaining how all the other prophets were killed with a sword, and then he goes on to say even I am the only one left, and I think my life should be taken away. Elijah is clearly in his feelings; he feels like it's not fair for him. Many times when things began to unfold in front of our eyes, we want to run because we're afraid when we look at it with our natural eyes. The battle seems dreadful in the natural eyes, and we can't believe it's happening. Back in verse four Elijah ask the Lord to take his life because he thinks his life is not better than the forefathers. It's something about when you're called! Doubt was creeping in Elijah's head. This can happen in an instant if you stop and look around too long at the journey, you must stay focused on the Lord. Looking to the Hill for that is where your strength comes from. When things start unfolding in your eyes you may feel like quitting, thinking thoughts as Elijah did, "Who am I?" that's a trick of Satan whispering. Just know that God has called you to a purpose and it will get done. Don't stop and look to long even when you get weary. God had a call on Elijah's life, and that's why when he wanted to die the Lord sent an angel. He will give you just what you need.  God spared Elijah through being slain like his forefathers, and his purpose was not going to be fulfilled in the cave. He was to go back where he ran from (Damascus) and when you get there anoint Hazael to be king of Syria and Jehu the son of Nimshi anoint to be king over Israel and Elisha the son of Shaphat of Abelmeholah anoint to be a prophet in your place. Here God commission Elijah to anoint others who will help him in this battle. We must remember who we serve. I must tell you as you are walking in your purpose, the attacks from the enemy are going to become fierce because you are walking in your calling. This was not only an attack from a few but a serious attack from many. If they slew all the other prophets before him, they surely were going to look for him. He fleshly had every right to run.... I mean that's some heavy stuff. But what's so interesting is when we want to run God's going to tell you to go back. We can't change what the Lord requires us to do. We have to make sure that we are looking to Him for instructions because looking at the situation will cause you to change your mind.

     My whole point in bringing these scriptures out in this chapter is to tell you that you're not alone. God will place people in your life to help you. Just because you don't know them doesn't mean they're not there. With God, you are the majority. Be bold for the Lord and be willing to face things others would run from. You must remember that you are operating on faith and not flesh. You are not alone, but in God He has you! In the Old Testament, you read of things that today seem impossible to man, but our God has not changed He is the same. What's happening today is the people's faith is what's changed. Stand and Fight for the faith that was once delivered unto the saints. Jude 1:3, remembering to keep our trust in Him and look at what's facing us with a spiritual eye. We must stay close to the Lord in everything through praying and supplications as instructed for us to do in Timothy.

      Elijah confronted all of these people that had chosen to serve another god with boldness. Don't take your eyes off the Lord! Keep your eyes focused, read your word and pray, knowing you're not alone. Satan will put things in your mind if you stop for a second. He will have you thinking this is too hard and you're all by yourself. Just remember Elijah and his battle in mind. The feeling of being all alone had him pondering under that juniper tree and asking the Lord to take him. He was called and chosen to do a work for the Lord, and that's what set him apart. I'm telling you right now these are the type of people that God wants those who will answer their call. When you answer your call, you're set apart. Be strong in this battle, keeping your eyes on him.

The Lord will have people to help you along the way like He told Elijah He would be his help. He had support and didn't even know it. Just like he supplied Moses with Aaron, he will provide you with what you need just be obedient. Remember the first chapter obedience is better than sacrifice be obedient to the work of the Lord and don't question Him.

*Have not I commanded thee?*
*Be strong and of good courage; be not afraid,*
*neither be thou dismayed:*
*for the Lord thy God is with thee whithersoever thou goest.*
*Joshua 1:9*

Think on this scripture when you feel like you're alone. Times you feel like you don't understand I'm telling you right now you pray and even when you feel like you can't get a prayer through. There should be some people in your life that have decided to pray and support you along the way. Remember our God is the same yesterday, today and forever. You are a piece of the puzzle, and it's time. I pray today for your boldness and your strength to stand against the wiles of the enemy and to make a difference in this world.

Chapter 7
Mental Strength

## Attitude

Your attitude is a big part of who you are because it is what defines your character. It's an expression of how you handle circumstances in your everyday life. As people of God, it is essential to be mentally stable so you'll have the right attitude and keep your emotions in check. When walking in the spirit your emotions and feelings should be kept under subjection while maintaining a positive attitude. Nowadays, people lack mental strength because they fall for most of satan's tactics. He is the father of lies, and he will play on a weak mind. He will make things seem worse than what they are, and to battle this, you will have to be alert in your mind to fight.

*Be sober, be vigilant; because your adversary the devil,*

*as a roaring lion, walketh about,
seeking whom he may devour:
1 Peter 5:8*

    For example, the suicide rate is increasing especially in our children. Satan is taking control of the vulnerable minds of people young and old. Suicide doesn't just happen there are signs of isolation, irritation, and worry. If you watch someone's attitude long enough, it will show you where they are in their mind. Have you ever been stressed out to the point that you were aggravated at everything around you? You find yourself yelling, and mentally shut down.
    Think about a mountain climber and all the dangerous situations he will encounter on the mountain; it doesn't look like an easy journey, because it's tall and slanted. He's facing safety issues

that will challenge him mentally and emotionally. He will have to maintain a healthy state of mind when met with opposition.

What kind of reaction are you having when you are presented with a situation? Your attitude will affect your outcome! Thinking and talking negatively in life will make for a disaster. You are going to have to replace that negative attitude and began to think positive using the scriptures to rebuttal the enemy. A few chapters back I informed you to study the promises of God, it was for moments of negativity. There will be times when you will have to encourage yourself because if you don't your mind will be filled with lies that will seem almost like the truth. If not watchful for these things satan will quickly take your mind causing you to revert to the mindset that you had before you started this journey.

I always say Satan likes to attack us when we're tired because when you're tired, you're not mentally thinking straight. You tend to make decisions from emotions. When studying a mountain climber, I found out that in moments of distress they will visualize that they are on top of the mountain. This helps the mountain climber to be able to withstand some of the most dangerous things that they have to face. In this life, we must visualize that we were headed to be with Jesus. Start mentally preparing so when you get there it's not going to be a surprise because you will be mentally ready for it. We don't need to let our emotions overtake us and mess up our destination. You need to be able to make sound decisions, and not having the flip-flop attitude. Don't let satan do as he pleases while going with the flow. Saying what you mean and mean precisely what you're saying. Practice having a calm mind, noticing that a quiet mind will allow you to make the right decisions. However, if you are filled with all types of emotions and a hot head, your decision can cost you the journey.

*But the Comforter, which is the Holy Ghost, whom the Father will send in my name, he shall teach you all things, and bring all things to your remembrance, whatsoever I have said unto you. John 14:26*

Trust the spirit to bring things to your remembrance. Using the strategies like praying, reading your Bible, and writing scriptures down will help. Quoting, memorizing scriptures, and playing worship music before the Lord is vital because they're going to change your attitude. Changing the way you view things will help keep your eye on the prize it will keep you looking forward. It's in our pressing and envisioning the top of the mountain that will make the difference. Visualize that you are there; if it's teaching that you're called to do, then visualize that. If it's speaking, then see yourself speaking. Envision yourself doing whatever you're called to do! Remember the mountain climbers will envision the top of the mountain when they begin to feel defeated. It all seems like mind over matter, if we get our mindset right. Getting our mind out of the pit and focused on where we're going regardless of what we're facing right now. It should just empower you to search for the strength to be able to carry on.

*Philippians 3:13, 14*

*Brethren I count not myself to have apprehended: but this one thing I do. Forgetting those things which are behind, and reaching forth unto those things which are before. I press toward the mark for the prize of the high calling of God in Christ Jesus.*

## Keeping in shape (always improving your skills)

This chapter focuses on the fact that you have moved on, and you've pulled off everything needed that could slow your journey down. I'm hoping that you've developed some habits to break the old cycle.

It's imperative to know the purpose of staying in shape. I'm sure you are familiar with an athlete who trains diligently to remain prepared for the race. He knows that he must always be ready in season as well as out of season. These skills are used over and over again sharpening with every mile he runs. A physically fit person knows that it will not just require the working out, but their entire lifestyle will change. The scripture tells us that to whom much is given much is required (Luke 12:48).

Many are working in their calling but have lost the stamina to endure. They have reached their destination, but it's not time to stop. It's a complacent attitude that comes when one has stopped reading, and seeking for wisdom, and knowledge from the Lord. This is a dangerous place in your mind to be in, because if you have let reading and praying go, then it only leaves one question. What spirit are you operating in? There are too many people operating from spirits that are not of God, because of this we have people who don't want to follow Christ. It's abuse of the calling that God has given them. What it takes to get there it will take that and more to stay there. Scripture reads:

*Not slothful in business; fervent in spirit; serving the Lord; Romans 12:11*

No matter where you are in life, and what stage you're on in this journey the word is a necessity, it's your input for your stamina. It has every vitamin you'll need to give you the nourishment for the trip. You must not put the word of God down! Pick it up to read it, carry it on a note card. Record yourself and listen to it at the end of your day before you fall asleep.

Prayer is another essential that you can't lay down. You must maintain your prayer life. You must know who you're talking to and who you're working for. When you started this journey you knew that you couldn't make it without Him, it's the same you cannot go further without Him. Why would you want to lay down prayer when it's what got you there in the first place?

In ministries everywhere, people have turned from a relationship with the Lord, and have chosen religion first.

> *Nevertheless I have somewhat against thee,*
> *because thou has left thy first love.*
> *Revelation 2:4*

Communicate with your heavenly father because all of your answers are in Him. You should've already realized that you cannot do anything on your own, but that you will need Him every step of the way.

Sometimes we get so caught up in everything else, and what we are doing on our journey that we forget to stay sharp. Sometimes we give up in the trials that we face that we don't even pray about them. If you notice you're getting overwhelmed and you're getting caught up in your work for the Lord, and if it's changing who you are maybe it's because you stopped exercising that new lifestyle change. It's time to get back on the treadmill of faith. Start back communicating with the Lord!

    The Bible is the living word of God; it will find you right where you are. You don't have room for falls, because if you fall this can mean the end of your trip. People that fall from a great distance in the natural usually break something, and when that happens, it takes time to heal. After healing you may get back up, but it will take time. Nevertheless, put your feet in the ground, and become like Hinds feet walking upon High places.

Chapter 8

**Balance**

Have you ever felt so exhausted to the point that you're not able to think straight? Remember the times when you didn't want to get out of bed because you're so tired from tossing and turning for hours. When you feel like this, it's because your body has reached the point of exhaustion. At some point in your life, you've thought that it was okay to push and push till you've reached total exhaustion before you take a break. You have a mile-long to-do list, but you're functioning like a robot with a sense of just going through the motions. Moving in constant overdrive will burn you out quickly, and in moments like these satan will play in your mind harder than ever before. He will drive all kinds of thoughts in your mind, and the fact that you don't have clarity at this moment means he's bound to shake you? Getting to this point means you've gone too far. You'll have to learn how to set boundaries before you reach this point.

    Setting limits for your physical body to do the work of the Lord is a necessity. Eating and sleeping are just as important as studying the word of God. You need time to allow your temple to regenerate itself. When working for the Lord, you're giving of yourself, and if you don't make time to replenish you'll begin operating in yourself rather than in the spirit.

## What you can do to set boundaries.

*Whether therefore ye eat or drink,
or whatsoever ye do,
do all to the glory of God.
1 Corinthians 10:31*

1. Eat healthy food as much as possible, because it can be so easy to eat greasy and fried foods. Try to eat as many fresh foods as possible. Eating this way will mean you'll have to shop on the outside of the aisles in the supermarket. If you ever stop to notice all the healthy things are not in the aisles but all the way around the perimeter of the store. Such as the produce section,

meat section, and frozen sections. Avoid the process foods as much as possible.

2. Drinking plenty of fluids to keep from becoming dehydrated. To do this, you will need to drink plenty of water, not just sugary, or caffeinated drinks. If all you drink are caffeinated drinks, you will become more dehydrated quickly because caffeine acts as a diuretic.

*Six days thou shalt do thy work, and on the seventh-day thou shalt rest: that thine ox and thine ass may rest, and the son of thy handmaid,
and the stranger may be refreshed.
Exodus 23:12*

3. Getting at least between 6-8 hours of sleep

4.   Learn to enjoy your family and friends, and careful not to neglect them, but cherish them to the fullest.

Let's talk about the mountain climber who is on the mountain. He is reaching higher altitudes, and the higher he goes there will be more stress on his body. Reaching these higher elevations, he knows to pay attention to his body to see how his body is reacting to the higher altitude. There will be times he will have to rest so that he can allow his body to adjust to the condition. When he gets on the mountaintop, he doesn't go running a marathon instead he's wise and allows his body to catch up. Balance is the key to success. The wetter and colder the mountain gets the more breaks he'll have to take to make adjustments.

    Observe the change in your body's reactions, as well as your family's reactions the higher you get. Your immediate family is who I'm speaking about, those under the same roof. There shouldn't be tension or strife in your home. A home like that will affect you more than you realize. There are always signs before this takes place. Seek for balance so that you're not so distracted that you don't enjoy the view. Don't be as some and make it to the top losing the ones who have labored with you. One of the ways they have labored with you is by waiting patiently for you. I've known this to happen because people take their focus off Jesus. If you don't pay attention, you will end up losing.

> *"For we wrestle not against flesh and blood, but against*

*principalities, against powers, against the rulers of the darkness of this world, against spiritual wickedness in high places."*
*Ephesians 6:12*

      Be on guard and take care of yourself by praying, fasting, and continuing to read his word. You will need to see the cunning ways of satan, so be alert, sober-minded, and not spiritually asleep. Pay attention to your body watch for the change in your focus, your alertness, sleeping pattern as well as restlessness. Are you stressing silently, are you getting impatient and getting irritated quicker, or have you just backed off and became slack? Pay attention to those around you that are on this journey with you watching one another. It seems like a lot, but with God, you can do all things. You have come a long way now it's time to continue to be steadfast. Look for signs before becoming defeated. Teach those around you what to watch out for. You must know that others are on their way too and it's important to pay attention to them.

    The work of God that you're doing is so important you cannot give up! You must continue to armor up.

## Chapter 9
## Your Responsibility

When the Lord calls you to a work, He has given you a responsibility that's for you. This means He has equipped you for this service, and you will be held responsible for it. It's amazing how we get so excited when we're first called to the ministry, so full of fire to run and fulfill God's purpose that it's hard to take a break. Now after working in the call for a while will you still feel that way? A person doesn't have to say very much of anything to know if they have lost their passion for their call.

One thing about our God is He is not a God that he should lie. God is ever so faithful! When He has given you a work you must maintain that position until he relieves you, you just can't lay it down because you get tired. If Jesus did that where would we be, he bared his cross up until the crucifixion.

We must learn how to stand and endure things, and not be so quick to run and give up but to stand for righteousness and be bold. He has given you the vision. Therefore, He's going to hold you accountable for it. That's why it's so important to see it to the end. He will send you help, but you must be mindful of their positions and know everyone's place.

Elijah anointed Elisha according to the scripture, but Elisha was limited until it was his time. Elisha wanted a double portion of Elijah's spirit, and he

couldn't receive it until he saw
Elijah be taken up (2 Kings 2:9-12).
Everyone one has a season but be
mindful to complete yours. It's not
your responsibility to give it up until
the Lord has released you, it doesn't
matter how you feel. This is why you
see some people going in circles,
because they haven't been released.
Don't get so tired that you desire
someone else to take your position.
What's sad is when we have given
our responsibility to someone else,
and we get disgusted because people
aren't coming up to our
expectations. We fuss about what
we think they should be doing, but
in reality, God didn't give it to them.
He gave it to you! You must work
the works that he sent you to do.
Those that the Lord sent to help are
up under your leadership not there
to take your position. Stop looking
for somebody else to do your job do

what God has giving you to do.
Don't stop putting in your time.
      The Lord has called you to
a work and others may not
understand you. You may even feel
lonely at times, but just like when
God encouraged Joshua to be strong
and of good courage do not be afraid
or be dismayed for the Lord your
God is with you wherever you go.
      Continue your work until
your season is up!


Chapter 10

What if...?


Now that you're
traveling on the mountain you're not

where you used to be, and not quite to the top yet. What if all at once things take a sudden shift? What if something happens and it's entirely different than the curveball, like a severe reaction to the altitude change. There are two major illnesses that a mountain climber will have to watch for as he encounters new heights. One is called cerebral edema (fluid in the brain) that can stop the brain from functioning. Another major illness that mountaineers encounter is pulmonary edema (fluid entering the lungs).

      What if a climber who's headed up the mountain reaches an elevation and his body does not adjust to the changes; his condition is getting worse continuously every step resulting in him ending the trip. His thoughts were that even though he comes from a family of mountain climbers, no one in his generation has ever had this reaction to the increase of altitude. This can be devastating, but he asks himself, "Wasn't I prepared? I thought I'd done everything that I was supposed to, what happened?" This would be common for some who would want to walk away heartbroken blaming God for a situation like this.

Let's look at it spiritually! You're working on your calling, and you've come so far, but you've reached a season where you have to go back down because of a complication that just occurred. Something severe, not just a curveball, or something that you'll have to take a break from, but a severe difficulty that hinders you from going any further. Not everything is the devil; some things will happen. The biggest shock is that it didn't even cross your mind while you were on the ground to not go forward, because all those you knew never had to encounter what you've encountered. For whatever reason, it's happening now; the question is what's next?

Fear didn't stop you from climbing the mountain. You've gone through different obstacles, faced your fears, and stood on your faith, and you didn't let it stop you from climbing. Now you can't let this sudden change stop you, because you're facing something new. You had the mental strength to succeed to this point. Now you'll have to be able to continue the rest of the way. When things happen like this, some people feel sorry for you, and it's hard for them to step up and offer encouragement. You will need to be able to encourage yourself leaning on God. Continue in praying and reading the word to keep your faith. Negative thoughts will show up, and be mindful to watch for the signs of Satan.

Even if you are in that percentage that has to take a step down, it doesn't mean that it will stop you. You must continue to fulfill the calling that He's given you. Keep in mind that the overall purpose is to serve people, and it's not about our expectations, but God's expectations! We may have expected to get to the top of the mountain, but maybe God has us on another level for a reason. This thinking gets in the way of what God wants for us. Stay focused on his expectations because our fear comes in when we start looking at the situation. You didn't expect this, but God already knew. Surrender to the one with the plan!

Many times we lose focus because of our expectations, and then when we're faced with a sudden change. We give up.

Expectations got in the way of God's will. Our expectations can be a gateway for satan. We're so disappointed in what God says that we quit altogether because it's not our way. Satan gives us thoughts telling us we're not worthy, and he plants in your mind to start hating on the person who made it to that position you've always wanted to get to. He will cause you to stop fellowshipping and isolate yourself because everyone is looking and talking about you.

When the mountain climber is faced with the decision to continue or to come back down, he chooses to come down because he knows he will die if he continues farther. Automatic healing will return to normal if he comes down to the altitude he can tolerate. Sometimes people don't know they have an underlying sickness until they have taken the journey. You must remember the lessons that were learned while on the mountain will never be forgotten, but that you can help someone else. The mountain climber makes the decision to come down, and he will have standbys available to call, because of the symptoms like slowed breathing, really tired, heart racing, usually they will have someone call 911 to get them off the mountain as soon as possible by sending a helicopter to get you.

      Discouragement can come easy; know that if you have survived God is not through with you yet. There may be another direction you need to seek for, so begin to listen.

      You got this far on the mountain for a reason, but don't let your emotions get in the way. There will be things that you don't have the answers to, but that's okay! Don't let your desires get in the way

of doing what God has given you.
You should not want to do anything
if it's not in the will of the Lord.
What God has for you will surpass
everything that we can ever dream
of.

*Wherefore let him that thinketh
he standeth take heed lest he falls.
There hath no temptation
taken you but such as is common to
man: but God is faithful, who will not
suffer you to be tempted above that
ye are able; but will with the
temptation also make a way to
escape,
that ye may be able to bear it.
1 Corinthians 10:12-13*

# Chapter 11
# The View

## Changes with success

If you speak to anyone about David in the bible at some point, they like to reference him as a man after God's own heart despite his mistakes. One of the stories that David is so popular about is when David has Bathsheba's husband killed. One of the most important parts of this story is when David is confronted by Nathan who told him a parable that leads to David's repentance (2 Samuel Chapter 12). In reading the story, you'll find that David for a brief moment lost his direction. It's so easy when you're at the top to forget where you've come from even if it's for a split second. That's all it will take for the damage to take place. David abused his position; he was seated on the rooftop where he was able to look down on Bathsheba. His desire put him in a position to abuse what God has given him. The Lord entrusted David with these people. Her husband was willing to be obedient to his King, but he had no idea that David wanted what belonged to him. When you have reached success or your destination if not careful with your position, terrible choices can become so easy when you think you have the power.

When making choices, you must remember that there are consequences for every decision. It's so easy to forget that what it took to get you there will take the same to keep you there. You must not become slack with your praying and fasting but instead become more diligent with seeking Christ the higher you get. No matter how many people you think you may have following you, remember to be humble. There is no power greater than God's, the one who has given you what you have. The people that he's placed to learn from you are watching, and yet the Lord has entrusted them in your care. Your calling is a position that should be handled with care, and this is why the world we are living in people are turning away from the gospel. Not saying that you're not expected to error, we may error, but we need to be always aware and humbly seek God continually. If there are signs that are not holy and will separate you from God you don't need to wait till the damage before you address it. He has equipped and appointed you to a work. I want you always to remember the struggle won't be easy, but obstacles that you had to face made you stronger.

      It's not about success it's about the people. The reason why you're doing it, is to fulfill the purpose of spreading the gospel. According to Scripture everything that Jesus did it was for the people.

*When Jesus heard it, he saith unto them,
They that are whole have no need of the physician, but they that are sick:
I came not to call the righteous, but sinners to repentance.
Mark 2:17*

    He's placed a purpose in your life for those that are in need of what He's giving you.
    Never get yourself in a position that it's all you. Humility is a fruit of the spirit, and we should not be proud or boastful. Knowing you did not do this on your own, but you continued to trust God every step of the way. He gave you the air to breathe, and it was Him that calmed your fears. He gives you the words to speak. Don't get caught up in the success. I believe at some point people with callings have had

good intentions and have started well, but when they get there, they think they're done. Well, they're not! Our destination exceeds this place, and our crown is not here, but it's in a place much greater than this.

#

## Is it possible to live on the mountain?

Is there life on a mountaintop with the extreme weather conditions as well as some of the highest altitudes? It sounds nearly impossible for anyone to live in such an environment. After studying the mountain, I found that there are people that have a specific DNA structure that can withstand the altitude changes on a mountain, because of this they can live on a mountain while others can't. This tells me that it is possible for life at the very high altitudes of a mountain. This is faith building! If God can restructure a man's gene to withstand a different altitude; He can restructure you to face whatever is before you.

> *The Lord God is my strength,*
> *and he will make my feet like hinds' feet,*
> *and he will make me to walk upon mine high places.*
> *To the chief singer on my stringed instruments.*
> *Habakkuk 3:19*

The Lord is your strength, and he will make your feet as Hinds' feet to walk upon high places. He has equipped you to handle whatever condition, distraction, or opposition that comes your way. Be steadfast and unmovable, because it cannot defeat you! You have got to know this is more than anything; if you haven't got anything else out of this book, you need to walk away knowing your calling. When you have answered it and surrendered completely to God He will mold you as He did the hinds' feet to walk upon high places. God created the deer with special feet made to climb places that seem impossible for others. Once again He's created a work to fit the circumstance.

You have got to have the confidence to know that God has got you!

*Although the fig tree shall not blossom, neither shall fruit be in the vines; the labour of the olives shall fail, and the fields shall yield no meat; the flock shall be cut off from the fold, and there shall be no herd in the stall: Yet I will rejoice in the Lord I will joy in the God of my salvation.*
*Habakkuk 3:17 reads*

It may not always go the way you think, but no matter what it is, you can rejoice with comfort knowing it's all God!

These blank pages are for you to take notes if you are at an event, or if you just want to write down something that you would like to refer back to later.

Made in the USA
Columbia, SC
26 May 2018